Molly Finds a Home
Getting to Know William Miller Through a Visit to His House

by Linda May Everhart

Illustrations by Maksym Stasiuk

Dedication

It is with special joy that we dedicate this little book to Alice Voorheis, who loves children, children's literature, and the William Miller Home and Farm.

Thank you, Alice, for the inspiration you have been to all of us. May God richly bless you.

For Parents

Stories have always been one of the most important ways that parents have taught lessons to their children. Children love stories, and they love telling stories about their toys and experiences. As a child, you likely had a favorite toy that you took with you on your travels or that you may have kept with you in play or when you slept. This book invites you to remember your childhood as you read it aloud to a pre-school or primary-aged child.

The story *Molly Finds a Home* uses a doll to spark a child's interest in exploring the William Miller Home with its farm and chapel. Its intent is to engage the imagination through the "eyes" of an antique cloth doll friend. It is a guidebook for children in exploring the Miller House, as well as memorabilia of a pleasant visit to the museum.

The William Miller Home and Farm is a not-for-profit museum located at 1614 County Route 11, Whitehall, NY 12865. You can go to www.adventistheritage.org to obtain information about this site and other Adventist historical properties. To arrange a visit, email williammillerfarm@gmail.com or call (518) 282-9617. We guarantee that you will love your trip back in time as you visit this historical site.

Linda Everhart

TEACH Services, Inc.
PUBLISHING
www.TEACHServices.com • (800) 367-1844

Molly the dolly didn't have any friends. She was packed away with a bunch of old things in an old house. Surely she was lonely—so lonely, in fact, that you can almost see a tear running down her face.

But then, one day, a kind lady named Betti found her and picked her up, and she loved her at first sight! Betti loved old dolls, and she loved children, too. She knew just where Molly belonged.

On a sunny day in October, when red and golden leaves covered the ground, Betti took Molly the dolly to her new home where she could be loved by children. Her six-year-old granddaughter, Chloe, went with her. It was her job to hold on to Molly as they traveled down the road in the car.

WILLIAM MILLER
HOME
BIRTHPLACE OF ADVENTISM IN AMERICA

After Grandma Betti parked the car, Chloe smiled as she showed Molly the sign outside her new home. The sign said, "William Miller Home." Of course, Molly didn't know anything about William Miller, but she was soon to find out.

As they entered the house, Chloe pointed to an old desk with a Bible on it. This was William Miller's Bible. Grandma Betti told Chloe and Molly that William Miller studied his Bible to learn about Jesus' love and so he could preach about His soon coming in the clouds.

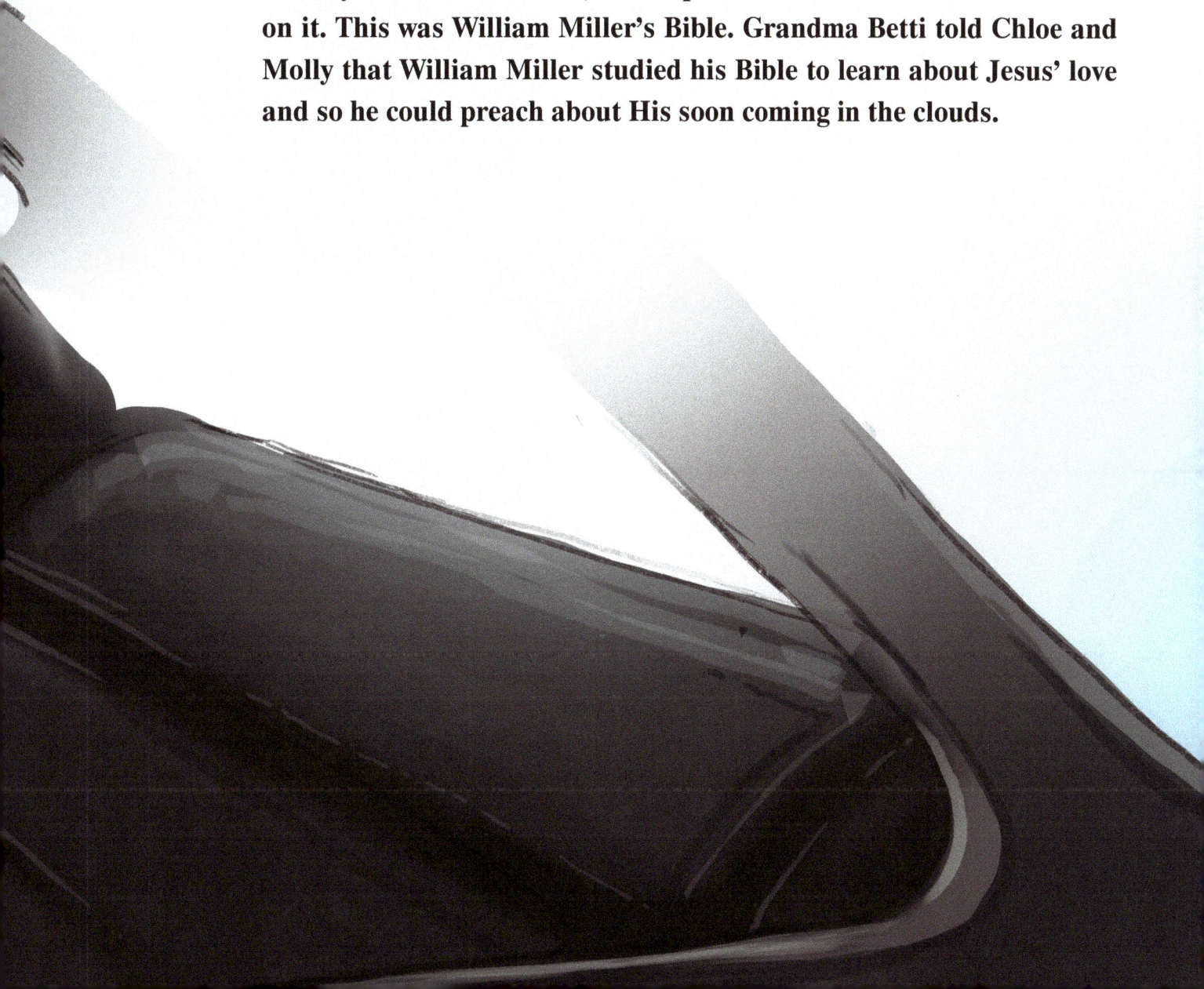

In the same room, there was also an old chest and a big picture of William Miller. He had a square face and friendly eyes. Chloe pointed Molly to a yellowed chart on the wall that had pictures from Daniel and Revelation in the Bible.

They also saw William Miller's big poster bed and his father's long bench that looked like a really wide, old chair.

Molly sat in an old, old chair in the room and listened as Chloe told her what Grandma Betti had said—that, many years ago, the angels helped William Miller understand the Bible. And now, they were in the very same room where this took place. Wow!

When they went into the parlor, Molly the dolly really fit in. There were old chairs and a spinning wheel for making yarn.

All the furniture in the room was very old but really fancy.

The wallpaper in the room had beautiful pink and blue stripes, and hanging on one wall was a picture of William Miller's wife, Lucy. She must have loved this room, too.

There were chairs with blue cloth, where people would sit, and there was a huge old family Bible that was too big for Molly to hold. There was also a big pump organ that people could play. Chloe told Molly that if they were in the house when the Millers lived there, they would have heard the Millers and their guests playing the organ and singing songs about Jesus coming again. Everywhere in the house, there was something that reminded Chloe of Jesus. Would Molly ever get to see Him?

There was another room that had a lot of things that belonged to William Miller or his family. Chloe let Molly sit on the Miller's old butter churn, which the Millers used to turn milk into butter.

There was also a baby dress that one of the Miller children wore, and there was a picture made out of a beautiful cloth design.

Grandma Betti told Chloe and Molly that William Miller had been a soldier who fought to keep America free. This was the first time that either Chloe or Molly had seen the American flag that was flown back in 1812. Can you count the stars? That's how many states America had back then.

Something else that Chloe and Molly found interesting were the flatirons that people used to make their clothes smooth. Grandma Betti said that they used to heat them in the fireplace. Chloe told Molly that it was OK for her to touch them now because they weren't hot.

There was a little store too with things for parents and children to buy. There were also games, T-shirts, hats, and even some maple syrup. Yum, yum! The syrup could have come from the maple grove right outside!

Chloe posed Molly with some large barrels for storing things, special books, and a scale that was used to weigh things like candy.

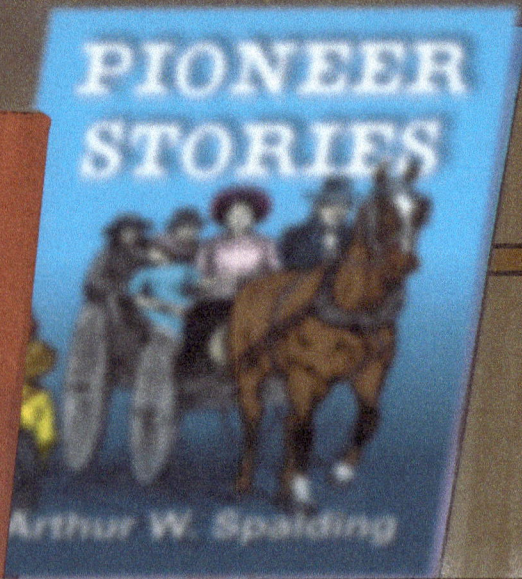

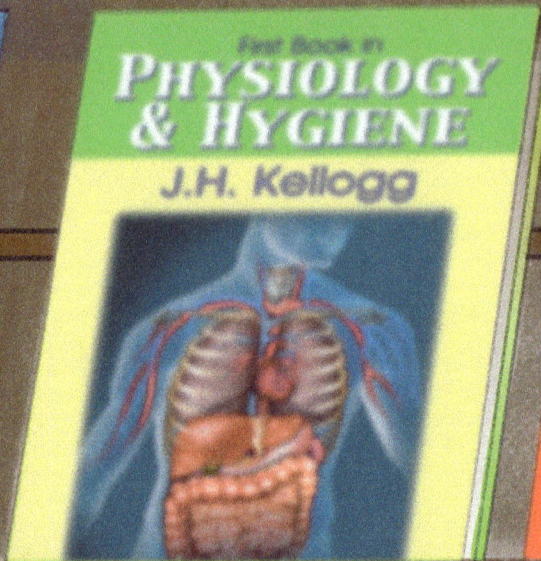

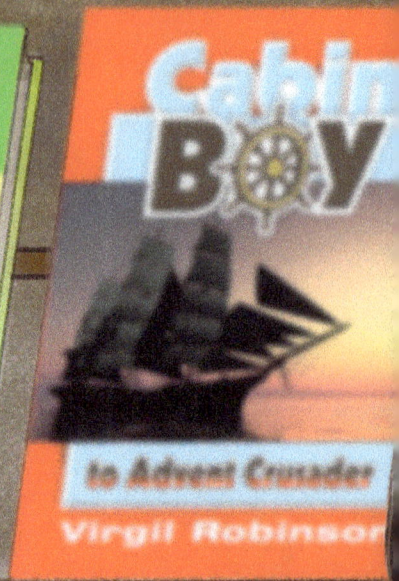

Chloe then showed Molly the little schoolhouse bank that is used to collect money to build a big schoolhouse for children to visit. The house was the perfect place for Molly to play a little game of hide and seek.

Where is she hiding?

Where are you, Molly?

How did she get into the little schoolhouse bank? Silly Molly, it's too small for you! But don't worry, someday there will be a big schoolhouse for the children to visit with you.

OK, it's time to stop, Molly. You've had enough fun for now!

Chloe picked Molly up, and she and Grandma Betti walked over to the chapel that William Miller built. It looked like a little church. People used to sit inside it on benches and sing songs about Jesus' soon coming. They also prayed for each other and for all the other people whom they wanted to be ready to go with them when Jesus comes back to earth.

As they waited for Jesus to come, they also read the Bible.

Then they waited and waited.

And they sang songs about being ready when Jesus comes.

"Keep your lamps all trimmed and burning,
Ready for your Lord's returning....
Lo! He comes, lo, Jesus comes!"

FOR AT THE TIME APPOINTED

THE END SHALL BE

On her way back over to the Miller Home, Chloe sat down with Molly on some big rocks that were on the side of a hill, and she thought and thought and thought. She thought about Jesus and about how He loves children. As she and Molly looked up into the clouds, Chloe wondered if Jesus would come that very day.

Chloe and Molly hope that Jesus will come soon. They can almost imagine Jesus and the angels coming in the clouds.

Jesus is coming soon because He loves mommies and daddies and their children—just like you!

Now Molly has a home where she really fits in, and she has lots of new friends. When you come to the William Miller home, be sure to look for Molly the dolly.

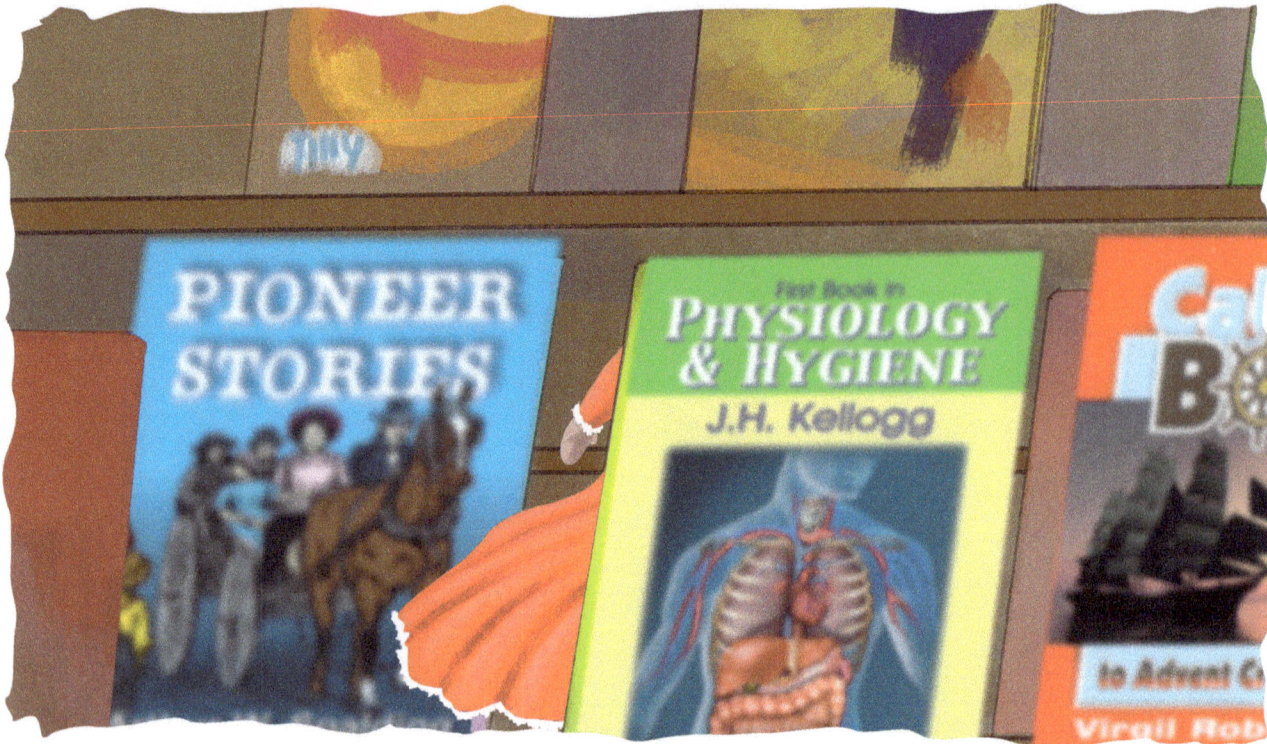

www.ingramcontent.com/pod-product-compliance
Lightning Source LLC
Chambersburg PA
CBHW061416090426
42742CB00026B/3488